domestic garden

books by john hoppenthaler

Lives of Water
Anticipate the Coming Reservoir
Jean Valentine: This-World Company, co-edited with Kazim Ali
Domestic Garden

domestic garden

john hoppenthaler

Carnegie Mellon University Press
Pittsburgh 2015

acknowledgments

I am grateful to the editors of the following publications in which some of these poems, sometimes in different versions, first appeared.

American Literary Review: "Bamboo"; *Blackbird*: "Passing" and "Some Men"; *Cheat River Review*: "Last Father's Day" and "The Gentleman Hunters Run Their Hounds"; *Christianity and Literature*: "Triolet for Joseph"; *Copper Nickel*: "Side Porch of the Elizabeth Bishop House"; *Cutthroat*: "Immigrant Song" and "The Garden of Eden"; *Great River Review*: "Deciding to Marry"; *Laurel Review*: "Domestic Garden" and "Vacation"; *Mead: The Magazine of Literature & Libations*: "My Life of Crime"; *Platte Valley Review*: "Prayer" and "Tracks"; *Poetry Miscellany*: "Finally, a Few Bucks and the Time to Travel"; *Southern Humanities Review*: "Checking for Ticks"; *Spillway*: "California Stars in North Carolina," "Holy Thursday," and "What We Find When We're Not Looking"; *storySouth*: "A Walk by the Old House Before Visiting the Nursing Home," "Drinking Alone," and "Faith"; *Subtropics*: "Eminent Domain"; *Tar River Poetry*: "Dance"; *The Greensboro Review*: "The Weather Down Here"; *The Literary Review*: "Chiaroscuro" and "Fable with Pekin Ducks"; *The Panhandler*: "Dinner at the Wok 'n' Roll Buffet, "Poem from Titles in Toni Morrison's Library," "The Short Visit," "Waterfall One: Rocky Mountain Day Camp, New City, circa 1975," and "Waterfall Two: Danny Holds Out His Hand, Economy Falls, Nova Scotia, July 2011"; *The Southeast Review*: "Sleeping in Elizabeth Bishop's Bedroom"; *Tygerburning*: "After a Line by Fred Chappell," "Camp Out," and "Red-Winged Blackbird"; *Unmoveable Feast*: "Message"; *Waccamaw*: "Anna's Garden" and "The Way to a Man's Heart"; *West Branch*: "The Whale Gospel."

"The Weather Down Here" was reprinted in *Literary Trails of Eastern North Carolina*, University of North Carolina Press, 2013. "Sleeping in Elizabeth Bishop's Bedroom" was reprinted in *Poetry Calendar*, Alhambra Publishing, 2012. "The Whale Gospel" was reprinted in *North Carolina Conversations*, 2011. "Deciding to Marry" was reprinted in *Poetry Calendar*, Alhambra Publishing, 2011. "The Way to a Man's Heart" was reprinted in *Poetry Calendar*, Alhambra Publishing, 2010. "Dance" was reprinted in *Making Poems*, State University of New York Press, 2010. "Home Movie" is reprinted from *Lives of Water*, Carnegie Mellon University Press, 2003.

Book design by Vanessa Branch

Library of Congress Control Number 2014943696
ISBN 978-0-88748-595-4

10   9   8   7   6   5   4   3   2   1

I want to thank my wife, Christy, and stepson, Danny, for
the gifts of love, time, and encouragement. Thanks, too,
to Jim Harms, Michael Waters, Natasha Trethewey, Shara
McCallum, David St. John, and Toni Morrison for their
ongoing friendship and support, and to Jerry Costanzo,
Cynthia Lamb, Connie Amoroso, and the rest of the Carnegie
Mellon University Press staff. I'm grateful as well to the
MacDowell Colony, the Elizabeth Bishop House, and the
Weymouth Center for the Humanities for residency fellowships
during which some of these poems were written or revised.
Thank you to Li-Young Lee, Campbell McGrath, and Dorianne
Laux. I appreciate editorial revision suggestions specific to
certain poems made by John Gallaher, Sidney Wade, Michael
Waters, and Susan Terris. I extend special thanks to my friends
Bill and Liz McGrath for their generosity in allowing me the
solitude of their house on Lake Anna, Virginia. I'm grateful
to East Carolina University's Thomas Harriot College of Arts
and Sciences for providing subvention funds that aided in
the production of this collection, and to Annie Hogan, who
allowed me the use of her artwork. And, finally, thanks to all of
my friends and relatives who've, for better or worse, made a
garden of it.

for christy and danny

contents

It's a kind of messy paradise, really, but
for the graveyard.
                                                                        —Carol Frost

                                                     If the garden

is not a garden, and if its tiny lamps illuminate only
their own darknesses, we must hold ourselves inside
forever.
                                                           —Keetje Kuipers

domestic garden

A ghost has disarranged these roses
    lining the walkway. Some greenhouse
        jokester must have switched

Jackson & Perkins packaging—*Heaven*
    on Earth for *Change of Heart, Black*

Magic with *Beloved.* I'll name them
    rancor lilies in your absence, though
        I don't hate you, & they're not lilies,

& you aren't really gone, except in the way
    presence sometimes contradicts itself.

Should they grow on me—fugitive varietals
    I never thought to plant—will they lure
        your bouquet any closer, spirit

away weeds I'll name neglect, aphids
    who'll stay aphids, sucking at the stalk?

I

the garden of eden

—New City, New York, 1965

He placed one looped end of a thin, white rope
between her ring & middle finger,
closed her hand over it, then walked away

with the other end until the line pulled taut.
Soon, wash appeared. A billowing sheet.
Boxer shorts, her camisoles. A flutter

of colorful shirts & water-heavy blue jeans,
cuffs nearly grazing the dusty grass.
He built a suitable fence around the yard.

Then they were both free to roam the property,
& the one sunny corner, & they made
a garden of it. Nothing fancy. Rows

of lettuce, carrots, parsley & melons.
He put up another fence—wire mesh
to bedevil hungry deer—but the two of them

passed easily in & out of the gate. Soon
honeysuckle covered the fence & drenched
morning air with bees and sweetness, & soon

tomato plants arose, & together they staked them.
Then aphids & a compost pile. & debt
began to appear, credit cards, a mortgage,

& then shirts faded, & underwear grew threadbare,
& wild thoughts began to enter their heads.
Still the garden thrived. Together they pinched

suckers, weeded & watered. When the slug jars
needed refilling, each would pour a few sips
from beers they held in their hands as sunlight

arced away into dusk. It couldn't be said
that times weren't tough, but they ate often
from the garden. Weather rarely let them down.

They weren't religious, but it pleased them to think
of that other garden. They'd come to see themselves
as whom you'd already guessed, & had gained

all the knowledge they'd ever need, as they saw it.
"It" being the gradual process of growing
old while their children gorged themselves on the ripest fruit.

camp out

A car must have clipped the buck
sprawled akimbo on the roadside field.
Turkey vultures have butchered its white chest
into hamburger, hacking their way toward the heart.
They posture and spread black wings six feet wide
like a flock of vampires flaring their elegant capes. Strange
how they always seem to be sizing me up, strange how they seem
larger than life. These things eat away; these things get to the heart.
It makes me nervous how comfortable they are with their place.
Scouts will camp here tomorrow, and they'll find a Bela Lugosi
costume party in full swing, the empty ribcage bowed
toward heaven, its jailhouse of bones too far apart
to keep anything in or out. The dead squirrel's
ignored at the roadside because there's carrion
galore and so even beggars have their choice.
The boys will pitch nylon tents as far from it
as possible, though the heavy smell will seem
to follow them, will seem everywhere all at once.
The fathers and the troop leader will feel uneasy,
quick to kindle fire and quicker still, hours later when
the sun has set, to squat around that fire and tell ghost stories
so honest and cruel even the bigger boys will begin to cry and throw
their marshmallow sticks into the coals. They'll sizzle and burst
into sugary flames. But it will be none of the things they saw or heard
that will haunt their dreams after reassuring horseplay and cocoa
have long since been put to bed. And it won't be rustling in the bushes.
It will be the only thing it could be now that the heart's escaped its cage
lodged inside of the arrogant scavenger's belly, has begun its turning
from bird shit into whatever it is that bird shit then becomes.
It will be their mothers who haunt them. How badly
they'll miss her and want to go home.

eminent domain

We'd moved into a farmhouse at the edge of the fairgrounds
when the court forced us from our old place
because we stood in the way of town plans for the new Super Walmart.

One day Mom swept us outside where two dwarves lazed
beyond the fence on folding chairs; one smoked a cigarette
and one was peeling a clementine. It was exciting for us to see

that the circus was in town. Life had grown predictable.
We were lonely and had spent the whole summer prying
apart dried buns of horse manure with forks. Someone had told us

that a county fair pony had swallowed her mother's diamond ring,
had lunged for the sugar cube cupped in her hand.
Our patience had nearly run out because summer was history

and school would soon begin. This was consolation.
From the distant side of the field we heard hammering.
We saw the big top arise against a cotton candy sky. The dwarves,

by then, were playing chess; a third had appeared to egg them on.
The sad one seemed to take forever to make his next move. Thank God
the animal trailers arrived. We admired the thoughtful elephant.

Hungry ponies ripped at the timothy. Two llamas took it
all in stride while a withered lion paced around in his cage.
That night music churned from the dwarves' trailer window.

We watched the one named Rico grill cheeseburgers. The song
was crazy, one we'd never heard, and Rico stepped back from flames
to play air guitar, flailing his greasy spatula for a pick. He snarled,

and he spat out some lyrics, but we couldn't make out the words.
We found ourselves sneaking under the fence to have a look around
before Friday night when everything would start, and no one

seemed to mind. The world reared up huge before us,
but the geeks were out there; our father had told us,
we could end up in their bellies.

Evening grew uneasy as Mother agitated the rusty triangle
hanging from its hook by the kitchen door.
Only the dwarves seemed to take it in stride.

They'd heard it all before and couldn't be bothered.
The lion was reminded and resumed his worried pacing.
The elephant shat; the ponies shat; the llamas shat, too.

We crawled back through the opening in the fence.
It was barely wide enough that we were still able.
The little people could have followed, had they wished.

sleeping in elizabeth bishop's bedroom

—Great Village, Nova Scotia

In the room that used to be hers,
next to the room of her mother's
scream, I'm staring at the ceiling.
My dream had begun on a wing

of moonlight, shadows in the room.
Across the road a car door slams.
All I hear from my wife and son
asleep next door is the box fan

whirring softly as a whisper.
But I'd heard the church bell clanging,
and I had awakened to fire.
I'd heard someone's urgent hushing

from the kitchen below. Mother
I could see in white flames. Other
than that, nothing is the matter.

home movie

I watch a Super 8 saved from the attic
when Mom moved to Florida. Tenth birthday.
Candles, a cake. My sisters, Dad's hand
shaking the camera. Brash light.

Uncle Eddie's straddling a chair. White
tee. Muscled arms, dark brown
from construction. His shadow almost
covers the kitchen wall. My gifts that year,

a Zebco fishing rod, a tackle box. Cut
to the front lawn. Uncle Eddie clamps five
lead split shots to line's end. I'm casting
into the road. One month later he was dead.

Chain sawing trees alone, bad judgment
took him. Beyond the frames,
I can see my grieving mother
almost losing her grip, her mind

someplace none of us dared follow.
In Romania, she'd raised him like her own,
now couldn't raise him again.
There's a point, a splice

more than halfway in, where the film
catches a little. I've watched the movie
six times through—and lost, each time,
those images back to where the end slides

out, slaps like a razor strop.
Then I turn on the lamp, snap
the projector arm up, rethread.
I'll rewind my godfather uncle, play him over

until that old connection snags, the screen
seems to melt, film burns.
I'll slowly reel it in again, sinkers
stealing through the uncut grass.

immigrant song

"Das ist kein Amerika," my mother told me
Uncle Eddie began to say after just a few weeks

in Jersey, *"Das ist Fehlerika!" Ein Fehler*—mistake—
land of mistake. Bad decision. Error. Misstep.

Wrong turn. Dead end. Comma
splice. Run-on sentence. Fumble

words—the ball. Drop the ball;
drop the night class. Wrong bus. Wrong

stop. Wrong neighborhood. Wrong country.
Failure. *Ein Fehler. "Das ist kein Amerika."*

My uncle died young, a mistake.
He made an error and he died.

waterfall one: rocky mountain day camp, new city, new york, circa 1975

—for my father

Top of the waterfall, I'd sit
and smoke a stolen cigarette.
Home was only a grayish blur
beyond trees and the curvature

of the world as I knew it then.
Fifteen-years-old—and I could spin
that scene, top of the waterfall,
into imagination, all

possibility poised high, top
of the waterfall, opening up
there, impossibly, and vivid
today as your still calloused hand

in mine as we stand together,
top of the waterfall, and for
once you don't plunge to the bottom;
for once it seems as if you've come—
to straighten me out—from heaven.

side porch of the elizabeth bishop house

The scream hangs like that, unheard, in memory
                                              —E. B.

Beyond crabapple, off in the neighbor's field,
golden rolls of hay are loaded onto a trailer
yoked behind a green and yellow John Deere.

It sputters, lurches forward, and disappears
into the rainy Nova Scotia landscape.
Other side of the clapboard wall I'm leaning against

is Grandmother Bulmer's kitchen, where Elizabeth
took her first steps. I can picture her grandmother
stirring potato mush on the stove; she's crying

into it, her silver hair done up in combs.
Young Elizabeth would pretend to *play a tune*
on each one of them so that her grandmother's hair

would keep *full of music*. I'm trying to pick out
Elizabeth's mother's scream from the gray sky,
but all I can hear is Mate's hammering

echo from the grimy blacksmith shop as he shapes
a horseshoe nail into a ring Elizabeth slips
onto her finger, *still hot, and blue and shiny.*

*

When Uncle Eddie died, my mother would not be consoled.
When policemen came to the door and she began to scream,

real horror shivered my eight-year-old back,
roused me quickly from the green living room carpet

where I would have been sprawled, watching TV
or aggravating my sisters, and it seemed suddenly

that the world was ending, some vital part of it,
and most has left me, but for weeks my mother mourned.

I remember his burnished casket gleaming,
the big American flag high on a pole, clapping

at the entrance to Suffern Veteran's Cemetery,
the army trumpet player blowing "Taps" and how

my mother whimpered as they let him down.
I tossed a fistful of cut flowers into the hole

while an aunt and uncle held up my mother,
muscled her back to the gray limousine,

my father, sisters and I behind. We followed
the black hearse out of the lot but lost sight

as it turned off Route 45. What we did then—or how—
I can't remember, but my mother survived,

nearly catatonic, for weeks maybe, until something
broke inside of me and I burst into tears,

sobbing, begging her to stop it. "Stop it, please!"
My aunts were in the kitchen, pleading, "Marichen,

see? See? Listen to Johnny. Listen to your son."
I was whimpering; I was screaming.

*

Follow tire-worn tracks around back of the house,
behind the barn and into the parking lot
of the former Layton's General Store. Take a glance

at the steeple plunging up and through
Great Village's red earth crust like a stake
piercing the heart of something refusing to die.

Flick the lightning rod on top of the church steeple
with your fingernail and you will hear it.
Gertrude's scream. Any mother's scream at the door

to insanity. It fairly sings now
through the corrugated tin roof of the barn
where Nelly has awakened from sleep, softly

lowing at its shrillness.

*

My mother returned. She slipped back into her body,
somehow, to survive forty years more until the stroke

and nursing home dementia that opened the door again.
Halfway through it, she spends her time wheeled up

to a dayroom table, spinning wild narratives
and taking no prisoners. A woman at the next table

she's named my best friend's wife. Everyone else
is someone, too, but never quite themselves.

All she wants is to go back home to Florida.
"When can I go? How is the condo?" she asks

to no end. "It's fine," I tell her, though, in reality
the place has been sold. In the hallway someone yelps,

then screams and screams. The staff appears ignorant;
they don't seem to hear her. Neither does my mother.

Is it all a dream? My mother's silver-tinted hair
seems charged by sunlight fractured over

Haverstraw Bay, flickering through the windows
behind us. I pray that her hair might be swept

full with distracting and beautiful music.
I twist my wedding band—hand-hammered, silver—

on my finger. It picks up the struggling light
and nearly glows. And now the clang of a bedpan

falling to the floor, and now someone gives in
and begins to weep. Pulled away, my mother

looks me in the eye with bemused curiosity.
In her distant kitchen, I'm taking my first steps.

a walk by the old house before visiting the nursing home

The crape myrtle & how it got there.
Its blooming seemed to take forever.

Keep an eye on every crack
in the sidewalk. The rosemary

has grown enormous. One might grind
a sprig under a sneaker; later it laces

the common room's stale afternoon air.
Your other eye is, of course,

focused on a godforsaken prize.
You'll break your mother's back & then some.

See how awfully she wants to go home?
She envies you the ratty sneakers,

how just now you seemed capable of anything.

drinking alone

in the nostalgia
of tequila
a face in the mirror
hung there
corner of my eye
or rather
I thought I
saw the glint of my eye
like when you turn
your head across the night
then double take
because you think
you've seen a shooting
star & in that moment
                    the blur
of light is gone &
all you can find there
are fixed stars
blinking

vacation

Past straggler palms
       there is a lagoon.
              Then there is ocean.

I don't want life
       to open out;
              I want it to open

in. Out
       is obedient conclusion—
              although the end is

variable and, face
       it, negligible—
              but from open

in—
       sifting what's been thrown
              together in our hollow

bodies, the dead
       and other remnants—
              can only come ocean,

lagoon, palms, eyes
       opened,
              out
of sand and salt
       and water, look,
              I've come

of scrub and
       buffer
              that is the way,

come tar and jelly
       fish. Luring from the jetty,
              I slipped badly.

california stars in north carolina

—after James Harms

I drove home from work, smiling for a change,
iPod shuffle plugged into the car stereo,

buoyantly inside the vibrant mechanics
of a favorite song, Wilco's "California Stars."

I imagined I was in Los Angeles, maybe,
giving a poetry reading, and I was telling the audience

about how, the previous evening, I'd slept under
California stars, how their faltering light

still managed to warm me through,
how impossibly happy it made me to say so.

Just then, a red traffic light blossomed,
and I looked up to discover, in front of me,

an ambulance, siren off, in no particular hurry.
The last strummed notes faded away.

I could make out a pair of ETs huddled over whatever
bones were strapped to the rolling stretcher.

Too early for evening to squander its starlight,
nighttime was carefully unfolding. West

was a planet, brightly lit,

farfetched.

what we find when we're not looking

I was hiking the quiet ridge of pines
beyond Lake Kathleen. It felt so like a church then
that I knelt.

When I stood again, when I was able,
I found a woman's Timex strapped around a limb,
thick as your wrist.

She'd been pacing—that much I could see—
and kept stopping at the watch's face. Was time moving
slowly or quickly?

Late sun rolled from the valley. Rain
would surely come. No one—I called out once but no one.
She looked over

nearly a dozen cabins, the bed and breakfast.
She could see the vacant day camp, the eagle's nest. Things
were about to end,

and soon it would begin. It felt so like a church then
that she knelt, stood up, took off her watch and strapped it around
the branch. She

meant to free herself from time. It couldn't last.
She lost her definition; time defines us. She was hiking
and lost her watch.

last father's day

The ride to Dad's was uneventful. I mean,
except for the squirrel, who seemed to have it in
for himself anyway, the desperate scurry
and lunge, the certain thud. But that was nothing
much in the grand scheme of things, and so it was her
puttanesca for dinner, and we grinned
little grins to register the irony.
Dad never flinched, and when had he begun
to drink white Zinfandel? Budweiser cans
were nowhere in sight, our mother's photo
was nowhere in sight, not even in a closed album
placed upon the Ikea coffee table
the evening before as a gesture
we'd have seen as a gesture. Where Mom's *Home
Sweet Home* had hung was a museum print—
El Greco's *View of Toledo*—casting silver-
blue electricity along the wall,
its cathedral's spire conducting heaven,
light humbled into dark conspiracy
with storm clouds, torrents about to batter rooftops
and flush the valley clean. "The dog got old,"
Dad explained, "and I had to put him down."
Did we want the boxes in the attic?
"Report cards, class pictures, 'A' papers," he said,
"and who knows what else your mother saved."
I threw my pellet gun in the backseat, too,
the case of bootleg tapes I'd play so loudly
they trembled the house with bass. My sister lugged
Mom's wicker sewing basket and Di-Ann—
that's how she spelled it, **DI-ANN**—
didn't like it one bit, but there went thimbles
out the door, tailor's chalk and the yellow tape measure,
tins of hemming pins, a myriad of spools,
dizzying arrays of colored threads, plus
the two of us, and Dad and Di-Ann
awkwardly waving goodbyes from the edge

of the driveway, flabby arms around each other's waists.
My clunker twitched into gear, leapt backward
into the street like a startled cat. We heard
the tearing; you and I both swore it was so;
the worn-out seat of the universe
expanded then. We'd heard it split a seam.

bamboo

"She likes the big Bambú!" He's grunting & singing
off-key like an idiot frat boy, shit-eating grin
on his arrogant George Walker Bush-looking face,
& oh, I do, I really do, but not the oversized

shroud of cigarette paper into which he's rolling
inferior weed, & not what he was getting at
with the double entendre, the largely
exaggerated dong lurking nearby, slinking around

there inside his baggy, relaxed-fit shorts.
I've remembered my grandparents' backyard, green
stand of bamboo, tropical playground on the cesspool
side of their property. I haven't thought of it for years,

how suburban New York became the jungle,
how magical flutes might be fashioned on the spot
by my bachelor uncle. How blowguns, how wind
chimes, long sunfish poles & walking sticks, & how

has it all come to this: barely stoned on shitty pot,
& the idiot butcher of Iraq chanting victory songs
& smirking, & about to fill my every hole with reeds?
Bamboo rustled like Serengeti grasses in the wind.

The skeletal clatter & mourn of my lonely uncle's
hollow chimes spooked the drowsy air. Always,
at dusk, a feral cat would come, & I'd pretend that cat
was a lion. I'd pretend he was wild & came only for me.

chiaroscuro

—after a line by David St. John

I am the something that starts out poignant and bright,
that enters the husk of your body until you become,

inside, a gut sack of poison and dread worse than snake-
bite. I'm trying to be a dick, but you know what I mean.

I mean, especially you, wondering so hard and often
if your hair color suits the sort of woman you're always

in the middle of becoming, worrying each frazzled tress
until it screams some response that doesn't remind you

of dying. Chameleon that you are, it comes as no surprise
that the sudden move to _____ resulted in a change

of political affiliation: birther rallies, rowdy tea parties
because you still fear losing what you've never really had,

and never will because the dying has already begun for you.
Can't you see it in the stroboscopic tattooing of *Fox News*

bimbos across your screen, hear it scream from your radio
as you nose the Escalade into a new hometown, headed

again for a beauty parlor that serves as well as a funeral
parlor. Once, you'd almost overcome your fear of snakes,

but you came to hate what came between, how everything
reared indistinctly in the muddled circumstance of dark and light.

You were startled by sorrow that came upon you suddenly.
To think, I am the shadow you once blessed.

holy thursday, 2012

Yellow and pink, and the greened white petals of Easter
decorate West Virginia's hills as I drive faster
than I should, winding north on 77,
and, yes, I've got on John Denver, *almost heaven.*
It's turned up loud, and I'm bleating along
in an earnest way, the world filled with song.
But Jesus is about to die. Vultures hover
with divine purpose, nearly their hour.
And, yes, I've got on John Denver. Almost heaven,
spring's giddy carelessness, its sex-driven
euphoria is mountain liquor, and the thirsty dead
will surely rise to wet their lips with it,
they'll savor sweets from the festive baskets they're given.
Yes, I've got on John Denver, and it's West-by-God heaven.

passing

I've just received a text that says a buddy
died last night but that doctors brought him back
to us with a shot, and so my friend is a Lazarus.

I'm in a boathouse owned by another old pal;
he is traveling for work somewhere abroad.

Mallards have lifted from the vernal pond,
and thousands of frogs are singing
because it's raining. I wish Bill was here so we could

talk about our friend who has gone and returned.
Crows call to each other across the lake. Same old

story: there's danger and it surrounds us. And now
the blue heron I'd failed to notice pulls his legs
free of mud and flies away. A small falcon skims

the shoreline. When he was raised, was Lazarus pleased?
I wonder how he lived the rest of his unforeseen days.

Were his preparations any different than they'd been before?
It's early March, and Easter will be here soon. Jesus, too,
realized how permeable the membrane is that keeps us

this side of death, and that the dead can come back
if they're summoned. The ducks, the hawk and the heron

have passed on through to somewhere else,
but the joyful frogs remain crazy
with song. A hunter's gunshots punctuate the distance,

a single crow lands in the crook of a tree, and it seems
as though the blessed rain has nearly stopped for now.

dance

—Kirby Studio, MacDowell Colony, 2006

Eleven moths have attached themselves
to a weathered screen enclosing the porch.

Like some overzealous bouncer, it's blocked
their flight toward eternal attraction, floodlight

above the studio door. Something insistent
& genetic draws them toward the bulb. Heat

& exposure bids them begin again the frenzied
celebration of time that's left in summer flutter.

Doing so, might they nearly forget what
came before, earthbound crawl & pulse,

laborious spinning, the fitful sleep—
sisters, brothers snatched by hungry

birds on branches? I'm sorry to say this disco's
closed to the public for a private party,

lone mosquito & his long-legged date.
How easily they shift from waltz to tango;

how pleased they seem for the blazing spot-
light, the rapt audience, glow of romance

in ephemeral life. But a brazen gate-crasher
buzzes my ear; whispers: *shut up & dance.*

the way to a man's heart

—for Christy

To sautéed garlic and onions I add
pureed plum tomatoes, a great splash
of good, red wine. Never cook with
wine you wouldn't drink, someone
offered, and we agree. I pour a glass.
Later, I'll add coarsely chopped basil
from the herb garden, sea salt, maybe
a pinch of sugar, and always the drizzle
of extra virgin.
              But now, as you see,
this extended metaphor is dissolving,
so I'm left with Pinot Noir and the glass,
fresh basil sprigs which remind me of you.
And now there's musing on the oil's earthy flavor,
and now this aching hunger, and who is it
who says poetry makes nothing happen?

red-winged blackbird

Agelaius phoeniceus

"Oh, Johnny," she said,

"that red-winged blackbird—those scary red eyes blinking out
from under its wings!—it's an omen." To me they seemed merely bloodshot,
accusatory—the yellow-ringed eyes a lesser demon might sport
draining pints at O'Reilly's till close. "Everything's an omen to you,"
I jabbed, scuffing at the dirt; "stepping in gum portends a mosaic:

Yuck and Litter, Bottom of Your Sneaker."
"Yuk, yuk, yuk," she said, "French kisses presage
germs, always germs—a sad, filthy dance floor at the tip of your tongue."

"But the damn bird"—
            I couldn't let it go—
                        "I want you to say,
                                    good omen or bad?"

"Idiot! That depends on his gaze—
not the stupid bird's; it's only a host!—but whether those eyes,
you know, **yuck**: if the fucker undresses you with **those** eyes,
you're toast."

            Oh, Nicole, I'm not afraid and nearly invisible; besides,
He's lifting now His wings, watching every flicker of your soul.
Yes, God's an abstract expressionist; here, a last ruby splash,
            final red take on a canvas He's dubbed "Heart's Hole."

checking for ticks

I flicked the barely visible parasite from your thigh.
We anointed Danny and ourselves with DEET,

roasted hot dogs on freshly cut branches, then
assembled s'mores: *two for Danny, one for*

Mommy, one for John. You and I shared
the last Heineken. At night, we stripped down

Danny to illuminate our revelations
with the camp lantern. When he finally fell

asleep, we undressed and began own examinations,
stroked, preened and peered with clinical efficiency.

And who will blame us catharsis, such affection
after this grooming turned quickly

desperate. We clung fast to one another. There
was nothing more to see; we'd passed inspection.

deciding to marry

—for Christy

The insistent sweep from the Hatteras
Lighthouse flicks over sand dunes
lining the silver-tinged ocean. Much was

made of John's expected shipwreck.
The rats moved on. The mast I cut into cordwood,
and fire changed its nature to wind.

I'd hunkered down in the last place on earth.
I drank from crude stills, distilled bitter fruits.
Mosquitoes swarmed and shape-shifted,

droned sad songs around my head.
It became so obvious:
you at the top of the lighthouse stairs, the red dress.

the short visit

The collection box is hung there
by the door like any other.
What to offer I leave to you.
We enter the house, hurry through

doors to the huge backyard, to where
someone has taken every care,
impeccable patterns, dark blue
paving stones wound through perfect row

after row of well-primped flowers.
We stop here and there to admire
such coordination and to view,
planted at the garden's center,

varieties flaring like fire,
yellow, orange and red, and you
and I shrug, then leave together.

the weather down here

—Washington, North Carolina

A quick stop at Food Lion for beer & whole wheat buns,
then Hog Heaven for pints of barbecue, baked beans,

& slaw. Idling in the takeout lane, I'm taken
by gangrenous clouds closing fast from the east.

In Beaufort County, storms are upon us in minutes; roiling
cells shear through the skillet-flat fields of tobacco & cotton.

In lightning's flicker, the family plots of farmers appear
visited by God. They startle me like you do, dear, like

Cumulonimbus on the horizon. Come gather after; slip
your hand into my pocket & kiss my sunburned neck.

Recite with me again the capricious
                    nature of our Carolina weather.

waterfall two: danny holds out his hand, economy falls, nova scotia, july 2011

—for Danny

At Economy Falls, Danny
clambers over boulders, heading
toward the top. Eight and already
he is impatient with standing

at a safer distance, so I'm
embarrassed into following
his quick lead and eye the fallen
log, the slick tightrope that's bridging

my own perch to the rock from where Danny
urges me on; Economy
Falls' roaring insistently warns
of limitations and the door

through which I ought no longer pass.
I summon my last nerve and cross
over. Danny smiles. Then he goes.

triolet for joseph

Joseph's mere presence confuses the gospel.
See how he haunts the nativity scene?
He is weighing the lines of an angel.
Joseph's mere presence confuses the gospel;
before Jesus turns twelve, Joseph's bidden farewell.
Stepfather met birthFather most take this to mean. Still,
Joseph's mere presence confuses the gospel.
See how he haunts the nativity scene?

faith

She stares at the lineup of men
who all look like Jesus
and finally points out the one
who most resembles Him,
swarthy and bearded,
a lot like Cat Stevens,
so angelic she wants to kiss Him
like a lover on the lips.
He is the only one who seems
at ease. Should He wink at her,
it would mean more than conspiracy;
it would mean that she'd gone beyond
the call of duty to finger Jesus
for his crimes and to love Him
just the same.

poem from titles in toni morrison's library

The Tongues of Angels. The Farming of Bones.
Human Behavior. Contraries. Easy Travel to Other Planets.

You Must Remember This. Rain and other Stories.
The Foreseeable Future. Voices in the Garden.

Anything Can Happen. A Handful of Stars. Grace
Abounding. The Dimensions of the Short Story.

What Happens Next? Unseen Rain. Hoodoo Medicine.
Breakfast in the Ruins. This Rain Coming. One Dark Body.

fable with pekin ducks

She and he were pleased that a brook ran through
their property, so they dredged and widened
and made of it a duck pond, which then cried out
for ducks, so they bought from a farm specializing
in such matters a pair of domesticated stock,

and though eggs were always laid, and what seemed
like thrashing duck sex sent white feathers flying,
the much-larger-than chicken eggs never hatched,
grew foul in their muddy nest, or they lay at pond's
bottom, turning gray as fist-sized stones. She began

collecting the delicious eggs and baked with them
her famous yellow sheet cakes and fudge brownies,
which she and her growingly detached husband
with problems of his own enjoyed with cold milk
or sweet tea on the veranda, which opened out from

their bedroom where sex was a problem. Country
life had done nothing for his ardor, and her clock was
ticking she kept announcing; *tick tick tick*, she'd chide,
tick tick tick. She dreamed of being taken from behind
on the settee, just inside the veranda's glass doors, crazy

sex from which a wild but beautiful child would issue,
and this miracle would so charm the fucking ducks,
she was sure, that they'd fight for their fucking eggs,
as well they fucking should, since life is so fragile, prone
to ill-use by the lord and lady of the fucking castle.

after a line by fred chappell

—Southern Pines, North Carolina, May 10, 2008

The girls and flowers keep changing into literature.
Girls and flowers always remind me of the sixties.

A May bride is framed by my window, trellised
pink roses in the Weymouth gardens. In the sixties,
girls hung out with the boys. Their music of choice

was rough but earnest. They fucked a lot, smoked pot
and protested the war. It helped them to feel better.
There weren't chat rooms; they talked shit face-to-face.

Maybe they didn't stop Vietnam, but they managed
to piss people off, thank God, like Jesus. Girls and flowers
is always the same old story, cropped together as they are,

May widows and funeral sprays alongside flag-draped coffins.
The girls and flowers keep changing into literature.

message

I could fling a carrier pigeon from this rooftop. I guess
it would fly, too, not drop

as would the proverbial stone, kerplunk. Nevertheless,
the world is a dicey proposition.

They are rats with feathers, the pigeons. Disease-ridden
and insolent, spattering

intentionally our most statuesque moments if left to dive-
bomb at will; to trust one with

words tied around its well-turned ankle is to be taken in
again by romance. Fold

paper into airplanes, flawed and risky; chance an honest leap
toward the origamic. Launch

them to spiral down or catch if just once that wheezy cough
of angel's breath. Sidewalk

gawkers will stagger, slow to witness. Even pigeons must huddle
awhile in shadows they'll cast.

prayer

You touch flame to the flickering idea
of a candle in mind; in a daydream
I blow it out quickly for awful smoke—
tallow from whatever sheep, cow, or human
become suddenly reanimate, this instant
to relive its final struck agony, separation
from body. If there really is heaven, then
open the flue. Alchemy of suet to spirit—
let it be so, & I'll light candles for all;
render up to You that which will burn; suffer
oily smoke, acrid fumes, the foul, spent fuel
of the saved—even the limits of light—subulate
flares wobbling, sputtering in their wake.

the whale gospel

Whales have run aground off Cape Cod again.
What if God created them for us as metaphor?

How like us they are, beached and prostrate,
sand shifting under them with every wave

from heaven. Bloated and murder to move,
they slowly rot in the blurry sunshine, victims

of distress we can't fathom. All we can think
to say is beware the giant squid, the seaquake,

beware sickness in your leaders. Beware the dark-
eyed shark, sonar's ping and Japan's traditional hunger.

The rusty bows of ghost ships
                          are singing through the water.

my life of crime

I stole the corn without incident, but it was
something I said, and the rumor spread,
how Farmer Smith shotgunned the dark
countryside with two chambers of rock salt,
how he'd tattooed my ass in a setup.
The ears were sweet, buttered hot from a pot
full of liquor. 'Twas the night before Christmas

when I sawed down your evergreen and strung it
with lights. I've returned from tracing
the garbage man's route; I've gathered
his tips and bottles of cheer. Yet, I've finally
found the joy of giving—here
the family, here the eggnog. Let's not speak
of candy canes while it's clear your heart

still belongs to your chest. Trust me. Jesus
and both barrels won't keep it there. The punch
bowl's been spiked; Santa's sleigh is descending.
Oh, silvery Christmas tree dripping with tinsel!
I'm stealing a kiss; I'm stealing the mistletoe.
I'm pulling your special star down from the pinnacle,
and I'll sell it tomorrow to buy the getaway car.

some men

Men who've kissed with passion the full lips
of women they didn't love, men

who've grown too reticent for the confessional,
who've cleaned public restrooms,

wiped menstrual blood from their walls, who've written—
then scrubbed away—vile graffiti from rusting doors

of shithouse stalls. Men who've grown
enormous with disregard, rolls of it bellying over

wide leather belts. Men who've been barbers
of the dead and were happy for the work,

men who've become what they've microwaved,
who overvalue the quality of their erections

and fawn over them as they do the town's new Walmart.
Men who look awful in suits, who've been there

and back yet grew impatient, men who go to wakes
to keep up appearances, who've made a deal

with God but can't remember the terms, men who are old
pros when it comes to hospitals and cracking

jokes at the nurses' expense. Men who wouldn't miss
your funeral, who'll kiss your widow with passion

and keep everyone's lips flapping. Men who'll move
in and disinfect your bathroom, who'll trim their nose hair

at your sink, conjure mythic hard-ons they'll purchase
at the Super Walmart. Men who'll kiss your wife

damned hard on the mouth, take off her black dress,
and have your Sunday suit altered and pressed.

tracks

—after Tranströmer

It's been many months since I've been out
so late in the dewy midst of nothing at all,
Whitmanically examining shooting stars
that shower earth like miscreant sparks or—
what—graceful arcs suggesting sex?
Last night, pressing a clenched fist
hard against my closed eyes before sleep,
ocular fireworks. But then the flood,
bright overhead fluorescence when
I realized my dream—hospital drunk—
and time once more for the phlebotomist
to draw. 2 a.m. reads the clock.
No moonlight here, and no fucking stars.

anna's garden

I.

Anna tends to her garden like some latter day
Rappacini, weeding, digging, pinching stray shoots
in a well-worn peasant's frock. She colors the gray
wash of living alone with black flowers, their roots
snaking soil, down and down, aching for the deepest
river. A clipped hedgerow of Sambucus blooms pink
in late June, spiking summer air with lemon zest,
and it's all she can do to stop herself from hack-
ing them off. *Colocasia esculenta*
reach six feet high, huge elephant ear leaves straining
for the merest sound of weeping; Black Baccara
roses offer up their velvet petals. Draping
the casket of dark tropicals, *Ipomoea*
batatas does what vines do—cling, and strive to stay.

II.

It's raining again.
Her flowers are black shadows
gaining on the night.

III.
Anna lives in the carriage house; the mansion she
keeps locked, electricity turned off years ago.
There's wasted space in abundance, and the heavy
drapes are eyelids shut against what light might winnow
through old-growth bower. She'd like to burn it down.
The charred remains would be a garden, too, blackened
beyond recognition; the ash—smoke-blown seed thrown
to the wind, just the sort of gift she'd wish to send
out beyond these acres. Haphazardness appeals
to her, in contrast to meticulous pruning
this world requires—unlike her dead husband's zeal
for order, the careful figure he cut looming
over her days like an undertaker. Not death,
it wasn't death. It couldn't have been; it had breath.

IV.
Under the black heart,
she squabbles with a blackbird.
He pecks at the fruit.

V.

Afternoon breezes shift; a scent of chocolate
wafts through window screens; *Cosmos atrosanguineus*
imparts its thoughtless seduction. Inanimate
as she's become—Jillstraw of her manor—such fuss
and feathers are beyond her now; the futile work
of its maroon flower heads almost makes her grin.
She's no fool and perfectly aware of what lurks
behind her desire for this cultivation.
For years she worried about eccentricity,
but later understood greenhouse cuttings, tubers,
bulbs stored down in the root cellar—she could see
that what she was doing was giving birth. Or rather,
what she was doing was enabling a garden's
growth in all directions and asking no pardon.

VI.

It's raining again.
Black tulip petals detach.
Black soil breaks them down.

finally, a few bucks and the time to travel

I, too, love spring's timely retooling.
This morning I gnawed on chicken wings,

tossed the bones high to rancorous gulls.
Tonight I've let my passport expire.

The only country I desire
is smoke exhaled into an up swirl,

the mutable shadow unfurled
briefly on my map of the world.

the gentleman hunters run their hounds

—Lake Anna, Virginia

Let's hasten through this early spring plague,
ladybugs whirring about on pitiful wings

while their homes are burning. Earlier,
two does clambered uphill from the lake,

disappeared beyond construction waste
we've yet to haul to the dump. Minutes later,

a pack of howling dogs followed, numbers
stenciled on their sides, antennae protruding

from tracking devices attached to their collars.
I wished I were a hunter in camouflage,

tracking down those canine killers.
What would it be like

to sip Armangac and smoke cigars
beneath their stuffed heads, bared teeth

polished and glistening in the firelight?
Some cultures eat them, I'm told,

but we scratch the fur behind their skittish ears.
Sunday morning, on ESPN, the celebrity hunter

murmured absent-mindedly as he kneeled
over the eight-point buck he'd just plugged

through the heart from three hundred yards,
stroking that same soft spot

behind the corpse's ear, almost whispering
to it: he was saying, "beautiful animal,

such a beautiful animal." You and I
are happier now that we've seen the error

of our ways. Though it is nearly dark,
coyotes will likely keep their distance

as we pick through our dense woods.
The last flaring of sunlight incites

the tree line into flame that will surely burn
everything to the ground, but I have never loved you

so much as I do now, yelping dogs
and their red-necked masters be damned.

dinner at the wok 'n' roll buffet

Guilty is how I feel on the road. Floozies sing to me
from the hotel's lobby bar.
Floozies seem everywhere,
multiplying as if I travel a hall of mirrors.
But across the service road
is all I can eat. Watch me
brave rush hour traffic and remain faithful to you.

A Chinese buffet is where the overweight take their last meals.
It worries me to death
that I'm here. Try not to stare.
Consider instead the grease congealed on your china.
Every trip to the trough
requires another clean plate—signs
are hung to remind you. The dishes are scratched.

Decorative rims have faded with the washing.
A Chinese Buffet is a whorehouse.
Still, fat people arrive. The hostess
loses her face. She whispers in her daughter's ear,
"Tell them in back, more
Kung Pao, more beef on a stick."
She dreams thousands of deep fryers orbiting Earth,

watches them glisten like stars. The fat people
change and grow unearthly.
Unaffected by gravity,
they gracefully maneuver space around steam tables,
steel serving spoons held
daintily in their swollen hands.
Wok music clatters through the tiny kitchen window.

She hates this dying from hunger; she hates how
her face changes when
she sees them at the door.
The fat ones; the sad ones. How the restaurant loses

money on them. How,
after eating their weight
in eggrolls, they rise, Coke-bloated angels, generous

tips blazing the red tablecloths as if generosity could make
up the difference, as if guilt
was a toll road and *here* I've paid.
So goodnight. There's ice cream on a chubby boy's shirt.
He's smiling, and his oversized eyes
are absurdly beautiful.
I've given in, my love, to desire so that I might die fat in your arms.

notes

"Domestic Garden": Jackson & Perkins is a gardening company, well-known for its roses.

"Sleeping in Elizabeth Bishop's Bedroom": Certain details of her childhood time spent in Great Village, Nova Scotia, have been taken from Elizabeth Bishop's *The Collected Prose* (New York: Farrar, Straus and Giroux, 1984). Other details from this collection appear in "Side Porch of the Elizabeth Bishop House."

"California Stars in North Carolina": The lyrics of "California Stars" were written by Woody Guthrie and put to music by Billy Bragg and Wilco. The song appears on the collection *Mermaid Avenue*, Elektra Records, 1998. James Harms' "California Stars in West Virginia" appears in *Freeways & Aqueducts*, Carnegie Mellon University Press, 2004.

"Bamboo": Bambú is a brand of cigarette rolling paper. "She wants the Big Bamboo that grows big and long" is a lyric from the song "Big Bamboo," often performed, in various manifestations, by Jamaican bands. In this case, the reference is via Cheech & Chong's second album, *Big Bambú*.

"Chiaroscuro": David St. John's "Shadow" appears in *Study for the World's Body*, HarperCollins, 1994.

"Faith": Cat Stevens, now Yusuf Islam, is a popular English singer-songwriter and prominent convert to Islam.

"Poem from Titles in Toni Morrison's Library": For nine years, I served as Toni Morrison's personal assistant. One of my first tasks was to reshelve books after her home was damaged by fire.

"Fable with Pekin Ducks": Pekin ducks, as opposed to Peking Duck (an Asian menu item), is a domesticated duck, the type most often consumed in the United States.

"After a Line by Fred Chappell": Chappell's "Literature" appears in *First and Last Words*, Louisiana State University Press, 1989.

"Tracks": Tomas Tranströmer's "Tracks" appears in *New Collected Poems*, translated by Robin Fulton, Bloodaxe Books, 2011.